Always the Trains

Always The Trains

Judy Neri

SCARITH An imprint of New Academia Publishing
Washington, DC

New Academia Publishing, 2008
International Poetry and Fiction Series (Editor, Roberto Severino)

Printed in the United States of America

Library of Congress Control Number: 2007940797
ISBN 978-0-9800814-1-1 paperback (alk. paper)

 An imprint of New Academia Publishing
P.O. Box 24720, Washington, DC 20038-7420

 info@newacademia.com
www.newacademia.com

For my husband Umberto
who made it possible
and for the rest of my family
who cheered me on

Contents

Acknowledgments

I'm deeply grateful to the Editor of the International Poetry and Fiction Series of New Academic Publishing, Prof. Emeritus of Georgetown University Roberto Severino, and to Dr. Anna Lawton, its publisher, for choosing my manuscript for the press's first poetry title. It is a great honor.

A first book gathers the harvest not only of its author but of so many teachers—impossible to name them all. But when I first turned to writing poetry, the book of my Antioch College Shakespeare professor, Judson Jerome, *The Poet and the Poem*, was my constant companion. When for some time I was engaged in things academic, the presence of Prof. Rocco Montano, with whom I read Dante, Petrarch and Montale, looms large. Back to writing poetry, I was lucky to have as teachers through The Writer's Center such poets as Merrill Leffler, Ann Darr, Elizabeth Rees, Michelle Wolf, and most of all Judith McCombs, who became a mentor to me. I also learned from short sessions with Myra Sklarew, Anne Becker and Rose Solari. Through The Word Works, Inc. workshops, I am deeply indebted to Grace Cavalieri, host of another *The Poet and the Poem*, now from the Library of Congress, and to Prof. Rod Jellema, poet and founder of the University of Maryland's creative writing program. In different ways, they both taught me how to discover, rather than to write, poetry. I must thank Karen Subach, teacher of a splendid generative workshop at the University of Iowa 2007 Summer Writing Festival, as well.

I am particularly indebted to Prof. Emeritus Charles Russell of the University of Maryland and to Judith McCombs for their close reading of this manuscript, to novelist Benita Kane Jaro for her insights, and to poet Gretchen Primack for her invaluable suggestions.

The members of my writer's group and other poet and non-poet friends have seen many of these poems and helped them on their way. Members of my family have contributed suggestions.

I wish to thank the following journals and anthologies in which many of these poems, or earlier versions, first appeared:

American Poets and Poetry—"Three Bridges: Postcards for My Daughter"
Annals of Internal Medicine—"Elegy for a Lost Toe"
The Innisfree Poetry Journal—"Angel: A Country Song," "Brookside Gardens: Butterfly Thoughts," "Go Away," "On Hearing John Cage's 'Imaginary Landscape, #1," "Don't," "The Poet's Improbable Wand"
The Country—"Chaos Over the Hors d'Oeuvres," "Antique Afternoon," "The Land's Look," "Brahms: A Transcription"
The Formalist—"*Teen Lovers*" (Finalist in the 1998 Howard Nemerov Sonnet Contest and read by Garrison Keillor on NPR's The Writer's Almanac of January 14, 1999)
The Lyric-- "First Child"
Passager—"Happening," "Impatiens," (Prizewinners in its 2006 and 2002 Poetry Contests)
Poet Lore—"The Why of It All"
The Poet's Page—"Watch Out!"
The Potomac Review--"Beachcombing in Sardinia," "Hospital Cruise."

Thanks, also, to the anthology *Classical Considerations: Useful Wisdom from Greece and Rome*, Bolchazy-Carducci Publishers, Inc., 2006, where "I Could Cross the Street" first appeared, and to *Secret Blossoms: The Art of Ability*, a University of Maryland Libraries chapbook in which "The Hammer He Could Not Hear" is to appear.

I. The Inner Café

Happening

The door opened—
it was the day
wrapped in sun-warmed wind,
inviting itself in.

Yes? asked the day
Oh yes, I said
so we slid
down all the slants of light.
We parted at sunset
over the lavender
petals of dusk
in a slow swirling.

I Could Cross the Street

and be gunned down by fate's fickle trigger finger—
An earthquake could seek me out and bury me
in a lightning democratic instant
with all the saints and murderers
on my side of the street
leaving the other side intact,
its electric grid humming hallelujah—
A killer microbe could inhabit my heart—
I could fall on the subway track
or slip in my kitchen and crack my head—
comic strip characters could
yes they could!
turn out the lights on me
just as I take in spring's honeyed breath
the winy exaltation of fall—
How dare I wait to kiss, to write, to call?

The Spindle

The thread gathers itself from the spindle
into stories, slips over and under as the shuttle
hums across the loom, each thread rubbing
wisps of memory from the others.

The spokes of my bicycle flash
in the promise-light of morning, swerve
down the alley around the cart
of Jamber, the fruits and vegetables man,
who hawks corn and watermelon
and the luscious short life of cherries.

My brother shoots me with his water pistol
when parents aren't looking. I counter
with a pea shooter or put jacks in his sheets—
We fight over who gets the top bunk.
Lights out, as Dad at the piano sends swatches
of Beethoven floating up the stairs,
he tells me that secret rooms open up,
with ping pong tables and soda fountains,
when the Little Man pulls him across the threshold
into the Cuckoo Clock, just as the hour strikes.

Pretend mother, I comb my sister's curls,
sneak her animal crackers between the carrots,
make sand castles for her to flatten.
When I read to her, I wonder if she

understands better than dolls do.
I decide yes, since she wiggles and squeals
from a tickle, snuggles close.

My mother, no teller of tales, collects
neighbors' inner lives over coffee,
plants each in its own garden plot
to be altered by the sun and rain
of her listening. Where do they go?
I don't know. I think
they flower into tomorrow.

The spindle pauses, as the weaver gazes
through bending light. She twists
the fibers of memory, and the spindle
picks up again, whirrs, sending snippets
into threads sliding through the loom.

My grandmother visits from Germany—
I am afraid of her. She wears black
and keeps the shades drawn.
She gives me chocolate but I want another
grandmother. I think she has seen
the things I fear when the knobs
of my bureau become eyes in moonlight.
Sometimes my father whispers
to my mother about boxcars, the smoke
of ovens.

Mornings, I listen for the needy chirps
of young from the nest
behind the house, a solace.

Indian maid, I ride out on my horse-tree
saddled in the backyard where the old mulberry
chose to slow and grow sideways

before shooting up again like an adolescent.
I meet my brave, who whispers tall tales
in the off-tones of seeds and the molded ochre
of clay. We build a tree house there, of rope,
scraps of lumber. He and I perch, limber,
high and hidden from grownup invaders.

I shimmy up the lamppost in front of our house
to hang from the crossbar just as the sun
sits on the horizon, then plunges over,
leaving us kids in a dreamy lamp-lit dusk,
the pale moon rising, our mothers
calling us home.

In clusters of language these scenes call
to be loosed in the ripe light of afternoon.
The clatter of dishes, the later, bitter certainties,
try to elbow them under— but their undertow
tugs me back and they unfold like wings,
tumble free.

Insomniac's Lament

Help!
I can't find *any place* to rest my mind;
every place prickles, denies repose.
Have to's and ought to's,
what if's and yesterday's woes
mingle uneasily
like Montagues and Capulets at the ball—
or landmines
dotting the shadowy terrain
of conscience,
ready to explode as I twist,
frantic for oblivion.

When finally my eyelids droop
thankfully
and my weary self
would slip into dreams—

No! That evil sentry
pulls me to my feet
and slaps away my sleep.

                Nightlong
I shuttle
back and forth in inner space,
alien worlds everywhere,
no place to dock.

First Child

What pilot guides your course by night, sweet child,
whose sleep boat ventures on the waves of dark?
You toss when my hand leaves your grasp, and slide
like a sloop that luffs in a cross wind, off the mark,
and then pulls taut; just so, you bravely right
your craft and set out full into the inner wild
of sleep. I'm left on the dock in fear's twilight,
tranquillity a luxury denied.

Till you were born, I never dreamed how vast
a sea of harms awaited without warning—
what landings do you sail for, eyes closed fast
and small hands clenched, your blanket's comfort scorning?
Tell me, do you steer by future or by past,
or only for the sunny side of morning?

Chaos Over the Hors d'Oeuvres

Chaos is in
they said at the dinner party,
everybody's talking about it.

Chaos:
the mathematical notion
that the slightest change
can turn order into disorder,
the circle into a tangled skein.

Dinosaurs could come back to life
and pigs could fly.

Just nudge that stone
one millimeter to the left and
an explosion will rip the planet
from its domesticated course
to wander dark space forever.

Any mother knows this,
how the smallest pebble on the track
can cut the thread of her child's design,
end the comforting shuttle of the years.

Now they worry
chaos won't stop—
everybody's talking about it,
how it wanders our streets,
                    wilding—
        O mathematicians, can't you mend?

Teen Lovers

After their fight, the girl and her guy sprawl
exhausted, each avoiding touch or sight
of the other, watching the ball game from the couch,
a humble host to many a tryst and brawl.
Their words are neutral, faces drained and white.
"That umpire sucks," he says, deep in his slouch.
She nods assent and notes with tired joy
the return of some rapport with this loved boy.
Sheltered in this truce they cannot leave
each other, dreading even more bad weather
on beachheads yet to come, with no reprieve
as surging waves of feeling tear the tether
of their young love. But still they can't conceive
of life apart. Frightened, they stay together.

Angel, a Country Song

for my daughter

I will make you an angel
from all the patches of my days
and all the scraps of my becoming.
I will take the bare, honest cloth,
denim to organza, and the rare silk,
all the crazy quilt patterns of my life.

I'll sew its doll shape simply,
stuffing it with tender things for love
and sturdy things for courage.
I will give it wings like harps
and eyes of burnished buttons
to catch all love's light.

Its brows will be arched and spirited,
the nose flared to take in the breath of life,
its mouth generous for kissing loved ones.
I will embroider it with my distractions
and hope its seams rein in my lapses.

Crook it in your arm and it will snuggle;
loose it high in the air like a falcon,
and it will hover there,
                          vigilant.

Dragon

My dragon's name is Kung Fu Tai Chi,
or Chi for short. I took him in
to write my words on the computer screen,
but he is as unpredictable as children.
He snorts in all colors
and likes to have his tummy tickled,
so I say "Scratch that" ad infinitum.

Just as a horse will test its rider's
firmness of hand and purpose,
Chi tests mine. Or—
he'll go along, smooth as smoke,
but then balks and declares
that he must leave me
to go for a soldier, or to rescue
some damsel in distress—
never mind MY distress—
or to take soup to his sick mother.

DAMN IT, I say, scratch that!
But dragons are very solicitous
of their mothers and will run off
to them at the slightest provocation.

This, of course, leaves me derelict,
for when Chi licks my words
and walks hand in breath with me,

we are Tweedle Dum and Tweedle Dee
and I am free to speak my
inmost thoughts, or bagatelles, even poetry!

But when it's late and he's funky, I say
Goodnight Chi, goodnight lunar screen
on which you meander. Go to sleep!

Anatomy of a Taxi

What, you want a guided tour of my cab?
This little world of metal, glass, leather?
Now that's a switch—usually people want
to get there and be gone, never mind me
or the cab! How come, already?
Having seen a lot of both, I think cabscapes
are like landscapes, don't mean much if
empty. My cab is a chameleon—it takes on
the colors of its riders.

                       Say I get a middle-class
couple going to the airport, maybe
an anniversary. Well then, my cab and I
look proper, gray tweed and button down.

But if I'd have the luck of carrying
an actress to the Oscars, well then baby,
I look swell, elegant as hell, and you bet
I pull out the spray deodorant, slap
on my hat, jump out to open the door for her,
drive nice and easy with my arms straight out
on the wheel like a goddamn chauffeur!
Naturally, I ask her if I can stop and get her
coffee.

        But say it's a druggie, snuck in
when I wasn't looking and couldn't put my
"Occupied" sign up in time. Then I'm

outta there, looking like a third world country,
wheels squealing, hoping I can drop him
pretty quick and he'll pay without leaving
me throw-up on my leather seats and no tip!

But you know, sometimes people
from the cab kind of linger in my mind,
something they say or they leave behind. Like
the lipstick dropped by that babe
I left off at Carnegie Hall and a whiff
of her perfume, a classy broad.

Or that other one heading for the Waldorf bar,
smelling like brandy and musk,
her purse empty, she said. Whatta line
she talked, just waiting for her ship
                            to come in, yeah, yeah....

                    Naturally,
you'll find the usual newspapers, notes
for doctors or lovers. Then there's my scarf,
for nights when my throat needs protection
even from the heater. Here is my mug
in the mug holder -- I don't mean no picture
frame, though I got that too, with my
license, just a smidge out of date, but
it's in small print, nobody will notice—
except maybe the cops. There's the lunch
my wife packed to keep me out of restaurants.
The backseat's a little torn over there
by a woman's heel when she and her guy,
a good-looking dude, had sex on the run
somewhere, who knows.

Then there's me—I dress in layers,
a flannel shirt, V-neck sweater, waterproof
jacket in case it rains and I have to throw
them heavy suitcases, hard and sleek,
into the trunk, skedaddle back inside—
it's a long night on the downtown shuttle
heading for red eyes at the airport.
Rotten life, mostly, but how else
can I keep those kids in college?
Well, that's the look of us, my cab and me.
Hope you got the tour you wanted.
Here's my card, call me.

Baseball's Body Language

The pitcher shakes his head and shakes again,
rejecting pitches signed in the catcher's crotch.
At last he tugs his cap and nods amen,
then spits and blows a bubble till it's burst
to warn the catcher he expects a bunt.
The catcher, also chewing, nods toward first—
the wary baseman shadows close his prey,
that runner, stretching out his lead to second base.
The pitcher, wheeling sharply to forestay
the steal, halts his windup in mid air
and sizzles one to first. The runner dives
and makes it back to safety by a hair.

The double play sign travels round the field,
the pitcher rears and throws—but till he does,
a dozen plays could mutely be unsealed,
considered and discarded in the dust,
before the real thing suddenly explodes
and a hurtling fastball meets the batter's thrust.
The small projectile follows Newton's Law
of action and reaction, while the crowd
now watches its trajectory with awe.

The game returns to batty semaphore
replete with moving jaws and lots of spit.
One thinks of jungle cats that seem to snore
for twenty hours of the twenty-four,

dreaming with their whiskers, tails a-twitch,
until their hunger makes them yearn for gore.
They sniff for signs, then rise to stalk their lunch.
The scent of zebra, of guinea fowl a quill,
the gambol of a fawn, provide the hunch
that sends the big cats streaking for the kill.

But, in our King of Sports, understand the fact
that chewing takes place first—before the chase
and seamless, flowing power of the act!

Three Bridges: Postcards for My Daughter

On the road to my old home
three bridges criss-cross
daring the thin air.

Three bridges link six roads
that lead to all the others—
highways seen from space
hustling to cities whose lights
wink back at the stars.

Others meander past Tobacco Pouch barns
and ponds where frogs kerchug in cattails—
places where life slows to a walk,
and laundry flaps its greeting
from rooted lives.

One road pokes me back in time
to pigtails and sandlot games,
the bell of the ice cream man
blessing the suburban dusk.

Another insinuates its way
to the center of my thoughts,
where every house and tree I pass
accelerate emotion.
I exited there from every day

and entered love—
until the light turned red!

Roads to bridges and back to roads again—
umbilical cords binding now and then.

Imperatives of When

For Ann & Phyllis and librarians everywhere

When I am carrying a banana and a thermos
traveling in a wheelchair
I cannot make a tuna sandwich for my daughter

When I am carrying a thermos and a pear
hurtling through inner space in that wheelchair
I cannot help my neighbor, who is sick
Or—God knows, write a letter
to save the library

When Moses, traveling, we presume, by foot
carried the Ten Commandments in his hands
he could not comfort the widow and the orphan
or pick up his son Gershom's toys

When able Helen's lovely face
launched all those ships,
she certainly could not stop the war
when riding in a chariot
or making her fabled jam

        Couldn't she, couldn't we
have wrapped kindness in a grape leaf
or consigned to writing the saving of a library
when traveling by foot or in a wheelchair?

Whether by Fire or by Water*

When I pass the cemetery at night
I wonder if the bones whisper
to each other, complaining of old woes,
vinegar grudges, their love-laced passions—
what Jones did to Velasquez, the night
both left their wives for Eleanora; Murphy,
of his job lost to that McPherson fink;
Mr. Katz, the grocer, of the thief
who spat on him and called him "dirty Jew."

Do mothers and fathers try to send
messages to their sons and daughters?
Does Mr. Henderson still fret
about his students, now all grown?
And Mrs. Santiago, the seamstress,
does she long to know the latest fashions?
Do they grumble about the wet, the cold,
the sleet, the wind, the wet, the heat,
the thunder and lightning disturbing their rest?
Or do their bones bleach in silence,
moulder in rain, as seems logical?

How little we know why we came
and where we are going.

* Title from the Jewish High Holy Days liturgy.

The Why of It All

I. Motives are always mixed;
haven't you noticed how
it takes a haystack of reasons
to break the camel's back?
Consider how she loved him
through sixteen seasons
because he was tough and tender,
taut and slack and because
he fixed her morning coffee.
When she followed him to Alberta
it was love of wilderness, not just
of him that drew her.
Plus he crooned "Alberta
Let Your Hair Hang Low" when
they were courting.

II. Motives are never mixed,
the supposed complexity
only a mask for elemental feeling.
Take the man who always knew
he would kill his wife—
the only questions were how
and when. He tried, over the years,
to mass the reasons against the act;
in slantwise ruminations
he denied the possibility
of ever doing such a thing

24

and so buried the idea,
an illicit, gleaming blade
deep in his psyche—until
he did it, with an ax, and perhaps
that too was clear from the beginning.

Antique Afternoon

burnished gold,

      whose fluted edges

         quickly corrode—

Could I but dive once

      into that glittering wind,

      I would live forever!

II. The Greenhouse

Go Away

Rain, rain. In mists, in buckets, in drizzles, in sheets,
windblown or straight lines assaulting the asphalt,
turning the ground to slip and slog. No halt
in sight. Enough, already, the plants bleat,
their roots rotting like war wounds. Give us air,
they wail. No, fire! cries the earth, whose green raincoat
is tearing, whose blossoms spin down gutters, boats
off to nearby seas or tangled in snares.

When rain pounds us more than three days
running, we think of Noah and dash to inspect
our cellars, wanting pitch and planks and a plot
for survival, as lightning and thunder ricochet
warnings. Wrongdoing? Never! We eject
that thought like ballast, and seek a celestial spigot.

The Land's Look

Have you noticed
how a landscape arranges itself
to please the eye?
It returns our gaze
mute, eloquent—
and preens
as we ride by,
its line of trees
receding and waving,
calling us back
as the eye turns.

Look
how it gathers
its shapes and angles,
its hedgerows and clouds
crossed by swallows.
        It knows
the way a cat knows
how to find the flawless pose,
arching and turning,
then settling down
into its nameless
grace.

Brookside Gardens: Butterfly Thoughts

At the garden's butterfly show, a paisley beauty
came to rest on my shoulder, folding and opening
dainty wings. I pretended to be a tree
or a rock and it stayed a while, clinging,
taking my measure, testing whether
admiration meant respect or a cagy tether.

We animals are weaving ourselves
into each others' lives, like children at camp
who tiptoe in search of marshmallows
over the sleeping bags of others. Not that the lamb
is safe with the lion, or with us, but deer amble
into our yards to graze, foxes scramble

from their forest homes, forced to vacate
by builders, and skulk by manmade ponds.
Crows grumble and squawk on our porches, berate
us in chorus with a hodgepodge of fellow vagabonds.
Soon, parrots and birds of paradise
will tap at my back door, with hungry eyes.

The Blankety-Blanks Are at It Again

Hear those cantankerous crows
squabble & kvetch! And lucky us,
they chose our place to hold their caucus.

Defaming their foes
in click, rattle and squawk
these wretches strut across the yard
with total disregard
for surrounding species.
When we stalk them,
and declaring war, fetch the hose,
their volume only increases.

Cacophonous,
they scream their motions,
pounce
on points of order, fly in,
fly out, requiring a run
of quorum counts.

Then, pell-mell,
in demonstrations even their own
sergeant-at-arms can't quell,
they rise and circle
settle and rise,
lambasting us with caustic cries—
        until—a miracle!

At a signal from their sentinel
their congress recesses—
maybe for mating? Well,
off they flap.
We *think* we're the victors.
We sigh and clap.

Think Green

Green grow the rushes—O! *
Plait me your grasses;
salute the flowering sage,
the vine's trailing sashes.
Hail to the olive
that in cocktails splashes!

Pine needles glitter
over nurse logs' soft mosses;
as spring saplings flitter,
laurel hugs the skin of earth.
See stippled leaves in water!

Crocs and armadillos,
a mottled green valley
from cloud chiaroscuro.
The burrow of the mother deer
settles in the meadow.

Green grow the rushes—O!
Scrub oak and sassafras
holly and viburnum,
desert's dun and bottled glass—
sea green, the source of all,
and from wild weeds, pizzazz!

*Traditional counting folksong.

At Herrington Lake

Morning rain lashed the cabin as tall
winds pushed the front through the trees
and vireos swooped from hiding to hiding,
calling through freshly washed sky.

The cabin too confining, we rushed to the lake,
light-spangled as the wind pushed its ripples
toward us and puffs of cloud rode the wind's whitewater.
We swam through cool currents,
then warmed ourselves like beavers in the sun.

Famished, we ate, as daisies, thistles
and Queen Anne's lace waved to us
and wood ducks threaded through flat bladed
marsh grass to beg for alms.

All day the light spoke its colors.

The sun flashed by the boat dock,
doubled in the lake, the ripples
from skipped stones slowed, widened;
reflections crossed from the far shore.
Bass rose to feed, lazy circles
bubbling up through dark water.
The breeze curled on the shore
to the slurry twitter of swallows,
and slept.

As the sun slid down behind them,
the pines across the lake rose
sharp and dark, told of shadows
yet to come, whispered: save this,
save this for a time of trouble.

Hurricane

When east wind slurs, insidious, in the leaves,
turning them backward, lime to silver gray,
the air will darken a shade, as with grief.
As storm clouds gather, winds slide in to play
a worried song, and creatures startle easily
before the storm to come; so madness slimes
the mind. His reason limped to a threnody
of yearning for relief;
                equations lost their primes;
his pages filled with murky proofs, an alchemy.
He fought off swarms of imps for his dream's sake,
while love came desperate, savage, steamy.
He pulled her running, aching, to the lake
to watch the sun come up; she saw their sun
totter and go down. The hurricane had come.

Impatiens

for Bert

It's an annual
she said; throw it out, it will die
anyway

Patient
with small things
he would not trash it
even though it was winter

He nursed it
through the short, dim days
its leaves few and pale
its stem scraggly
translucent like her mother's skin
at the end

She knew she was safe, too
when in spring
came one impossible
blossom after another

Dry Leaves

flutter wildly
in a sudden shaft of light
like a wake in the water—
one of those late afternoon lights
that tell you something has died,
the air a mortal clarity.

Did a key turn on my past?
Did another face freeze into a frame?
Perhaps the thread of an old love
ran out,
diminishing the tapestry
as the design came clear.

Beachcombing in Sardinia

Juniper and gentian
line my path to the cove;
the heady scents of
lavender, thyme and rosemary
surround sinuous rocks
sculpted by rival winds —
levante, scirocco, maestrale.

To the north
where the cliffs of *Capo Falcone*
plummet into the azure sea,
where the waves write
curving lines of an ancient language
and sun-splashed reefs
rise up
to claim the sea,
there, on this island of Ariel,
windswept beaches call me
to comb their sands
for talismans.

Barefoot, I wander
searching the littoral for secrets,
lost in its flow.
Its stones point to places
words do not reach

In the mind always
I'll find those sunlit places
islands in time
where a presence older than history
murmurs like waves
         on inner sands.

SURFINGthefuture.com

   ~Birds, move over, WE'RE here

   ~Our canyons are steel now
   their uniform geometries
   built to keep the random at bay

**~The Line For The Rain Forest
      forms to the Right**

            ~There's not a place in the world
            this car can't go! For a free trial,
            catch us at wildcar.com

   *~I remember the cranes—
   how they stepped daintily
   through the fog—*

            ~Fog is out, chump,
                  smog's in

            *~The map has filled up, my dear
                  and everywhere
                  is anywhere*

~The world is my banker
      I shall not want

            ~Watch the woods
            shrink to shrubbery,
            the gardens to pots!

~The dolphins are dying
Silence is murder
To sign the petition
email <u>adam@thoreau.org</u>

~UH-oh, too much us—
too few them

~When we sold mother's garden,
I buried my face in the apple blossoms

      ~People everywhere
      clearing tiny plots
      guarding them like scarecrows

   ~Previously used planet
   still good in spots
   up for quick sale
   at Universal Supermart
   email <u>everyman@noahsark.gov</u>

~Oh Toto, everything will be all right
      won't it?

        ~I remember the autumn air
        crisp as pears. When
        we raked leaves into piles,
        children jumped into them—

   ~Ooh the children
   legs like bamboo
   tummies like gourds
   empty, empty
   tum ta tum tum

~See the earth receding!
A prune, a raisin
imploding

~Control's the thing—
Who's in charge?

III. Out of Airy Nothing, Worlds

Writing

for Elisabetta

It's like combing the hair
of a young girl. First you have to
catch her, for she suddenly enters
your life, right in the middle of cooking
a dinner, or meeting a lover—you really
don't have time for her, but there she is,
so you hold her between your knees,
grab a comb and begin to pull it through
those long strands, tangled
from dodge ball and rolling down a grassy
hill. You get one run-through, but still
there are knots, some stubborn,
needing careful combing
so you don't hurt her, so she doesn't
push away before you have finished.

You return over the same paths,
the comb now sliding easily through her hair.
You think you are done, but then
perhaps she wants braids or a ponytail
or maybe a chignon like her older sister.
Now she sits on your lap, happy to be
fussed over, looking into the mirror
until you say: my dear,
how lovely you look! Off you go,
let the world admire you!

The Transformation

Apollo and Daphne
by Gian Lorenzo Bernini (1598 - 1680)
Villa Borghese Gallery, Rome

Mostly, gods hide from us.

But sometimes they break out
and burn, and we are dry sticks
in their path.
Then we turn and flee
like Daphne from Apollo.

How lovely they are, so near,
their marble forms almost conjoined,
yet Daphne is running,
her lithe body arched away
from Apollo's longing.
He reaches, a hand to her flank,
expecting easy conquest.

She pulls away in anguish,
desiring only Leucippus, her lover.
As she reaches the precipice,
she flings her arms upward,
mouth open, eyes wide with fear.

Does Apollo turn her into a laurel
or does she do it herself?
Leaves grow out of her hands,

a branch pushes against his groin,
the bark encircles her
to deny his flaming touch.

IN ITALY the dust

                           settles quickly on every floor,
be it tile or marble. It is the dust of ages and it must be
moved every day by broom and bucket and *lo straccio,*
the sturdy, wet rag moved purposefully over the floors
by a toothy mop. Women do this daily under the blank,
watchful eyes of pagan statues, or crosses, or engravings
on sacred walls or columns backed by umbrella pines,
the famous pines of Rome. It must be done to allow
the day's *allegria* to sparkle with the incandescence
of lovers' greetings, or the heat of ancient rancors.

Then the day can happen. The goats can go to pasture,
seeking the shade, as every automobile driver
has learned to do, following their example. Everyone
moves to the day's rhythm, the shopkeepers,
the horn blowers in cars and on motorcycles,
the gardeners in the *orti,* where vegetables swell
in the sun, waiting for cooks to handle them artfully.
In the formal gardens, fountains splash and the eye
searches the symmetry of hedges and sundials, the statues
changing hue as the sun moves.

                           Then comes the glow
of sunset on the warm orange *palazzi* with their
windows framed in white marble, the banners
of clothes on lines crossing the tiny byways.

The late afternoon belongs to Horace. Its light
tells of earth's bounty cultivated and savored,
the wine poured, the second nature of talk
and writing—that inhabit the dust which every day
must be moved in homage.

The Poet Exiled from Love

On Hearing Schubert's *Trio #2, opus 100*

All morning his pen dashes across the page,
racing to capture the iridescent flow
that wells from inner springs.

The *Allegro vivace* finished,
he slides into the corner café
for coffee, pastry and schnapps.
He watches the girls,
their bustle and flutter.
They turn their backs when he looks
too long. "Tubby," they snicker.
He pulls out a huge handkerchief,
blows his nose so the waiter won't notice
the tears. He longs for a dark woman in a dark room
but dares not go. Tonight, he will dazzle his friends,
a *Schubertiad!* Comfort there.

Sweet Franz: Flaming sunsets turning to indigo.
The soldiers who march below his window,
brass buttons flashing their pride. The couples
who swirl by him and flirt as he plays,
the sinewed hand urgent against the small
of her back. He puts in their trysts,
their mementos, the promises
they mean to keep. All that haunts us
wanders through the strings, leaps
from the keys.

Biography can never *explain* genius —
just tiptoes past the footman at its portal.

Brahms: a Transcription

Andante

Renoir's revelers sway in A minor,
winding through the scrim of time,
their children in laces on the lawn.
Primness seeks passion as the picnic begins;
the basket of bread and wine and cheese
spills its sacramental promise.

Adagio

The late afternoon sun in autumn,
the ferry in a goldenrod shimmer
as it pulls away from the shore
into deep azure knowing,
and deeper unknowing,
the self longing to sing
all the airs the wind plays.

Appassionato

Women pace in one-room cabins, in palaces,
husbands and lovers on tall ships,
full sails scudding under a wild wind.
The captain dares the exultant waves
that draw them on through the trackless sea.

The Hammer He Could Not Hear

Listening to Beethoven's *Hammerklavier*
Sonata, Opus 106

Adagio sostenuto

A guttering candle reveals the lined face,
the head bent over the keys.
In his mind's ear he hears the notes,
a quicksilver palette of light. He wants
to call back the loves who have left him,
his nimble fingers stroking their thighs,
the black and white silk of their dresses—

Oh, you will stay, won't you, as long as I play?
I will turn every chord into rolling spells,
calling you back. Listen, you will see
the drops as they fall from the icicles
outside your window, warmed by the spring sun.
They are like bells calling the swallows
back to nest in the linden trees. Now
the swallows trill their loves, *obbligato*—
the discord you hear is their mad screech
at rivals –how well I understand them!

Ah, these jewels on your hand,
the lace that makes your neck
so beguiling—I hear voices
calling me again, my music
embracing each moment
as a fountain
holds the essence of water.

The Nameless Lover

On Hearing the *Fantasy in Memory*
of a Beloved Place by Peter Ilyich Tchaikovsky

He saw the loved form
again that autumn
shaped by the opening of the trees
as he walked the path,
now dappled with copper, red and mauve.
            He remembered
their first encounter, the restaurant draped in damask
to which they came with others. They did not meet,
but knew their lives had changed.

Then came the note in an unknown
but somehow familiar hand, the y's dropped
in a flourish. His answer—shy, halting
yet imperious. Yes, he was married,
And you?
          It was winter when they met
in the Café des Beaux Arts.
Both chose the hot spiced wine
and their legs touched under the table.

They next met at an all-Russian concert
where one of his pieces was played.
They became lovers, meeting always
at a different hotel or country inn,
one near here. In the spring
they took this very path, whistling back
to the birds. Only an occasional farmer
or woodsman saw them. At dances,

they watched each other
with other partners as the waltz
swirled around the room, making
each heady with desire.

That summer they discovered the cave,
a five-minute trek through the undergrowth
from the path. They always went separately
and left alone, the cave muffling their happy cries.

One day the furtive movement of his beloved,
leaving, caught the eye of a hunter,
whose aim was unerring.
As the hunter ran, lost and away
from his fallen prey, finally throwing
his rifle into the river,
he fled deep into the cave,
moaning no, no, no—and flung
himself on their bed of leaves.

Now, following the path this autumn,
branches reported under his foot,
the leaves underneath the broken branches
somehow always mottled red. He went home,
locked his door and sobbed for days.
Perhaps then, drained, desperate, he penned
this *Fantasy* to honor their love.
As his quill scratched the church bells
onto the staff, he wept again.

On Hearing John Cage's Imaginary Landscape #1

Signs cross the city
washed in surf
as the time of offices and banks
pulses, sags and is silenced.
Bank time is transformed
into the psalm of trilobites
pinging in imaginary measures.
The sirens go meditative
then scared as the waves menace.
The lone tones of survival
join, walk the verge. Trilobites
become frogs jumping from stone
to stone of a primeval lake.
Both sound and silence mean.

Watch Out!

Poetry is dangerous: it hides
in the corners of the mind
where truth lurks, ready to spring—
it opens old canisters, slices
alluring fruits, with consequences
perilous for humankind;
it leads us to booby traps
unsuspected in its charming tune.

Sometimes
it lulls us to sleep
with songs of yesteryear, comfort
and rhymes. Old coin, smooth, reliable.
It can dance too, ballet or modern,
or with a child's awkward grace.
                              Don't imagine
poetry only tells the truth—
this rogue lies abundantly, keeps
bad company, drinks and smokes.
Still, we kiss the embroidered hem,
hoping to glimpse some Eldorado
and last beyond ourselves.

Aeolus Fantasia

I. It starts out quietly, with a whistle after breakfast
as he walks the path down to the sea. He tosses
that off to Pan.
              A family affair, his wife watches
the thermometers, tests the waters, sends him
constant lightmails. His daughters check
the lizards draped on rocks, the birds wheeling
and dashing off to their destinations, imprinted
by Time, in cahoots with Apollo.
At a signal, his sons man the bellows.
He watches the light in its daily battle with clouds,
then looses the white horses of the sea. He talks
with Time, sends up a lick of breeze. Underneath it all,
he listens to the deep basses of continental drift,
the slow continuo of mountains rising. Here and there
a volcano goes off. Trumpet blasts needed.

II. Mrs. Eos Aeolus hangs out a thousand reeds
for her husband to blow upon. Grasses loose and braided,
vines and tendrils, thongs, the harnesses
of farm animals with their bells, the worn out
nets of fishermen, the ribbons from her hair,
corn silk, even the filaments of spider webs.

Aeolus wanders through this forest,
blowing, plucking, dreamy at first
but then wildly twisting and turning

as his own winds circle and toss him about.
He skips down the path to the sea,
tapping on the shells of tortoises, rubbing
lizards' scales, until he reaches
the sea conches that call for his breath.

Chords reach the clouds and set them
waltzing. Apollo peeks down between them
and smiles, desiring one of the daughters
of the wind god, wanting to reach down
from his chariot and snatch her—
the day pauses, swings in the balance,
treble and bass lap against one another.

What happens when the reeds slip askant?

Aeolus is drunk, the day gone gray and sour.
Eos shudders, knowing her husband will return
like a mean, cutting wind from the east,
and she will feel his pain, keep the bruises
for weeks, those deep purple sunsets. No love
that night. She hides the children.

III. Sometimes he strikes the stumps so strangely
a new god is proclaimed and rises to Olympus.
Or a hero mauled in his winds ascends
to plead his cause to warring judges.
Aeolus must learn new ways to stoke his fire,
pump his bellows, sweetly for a Floristan,
cross and moody for a Eusebius. This has been
the range for aeons but Aeolus is aging,
starting to notice some changes. The corals
have shrunk, the trill of currents running
through them has lost its vibrato, the sky
glowers the charcoal of burnt fires, sullen.

IV. There are still days when Apollo's gaze is light
and his touch tender on the seahorse waves
that tremble as they curl with desire. Days when
Aeolus laughs, and whales and dolphins rise
from the deep, like mystic chords. Their arch
is alpha and omega, and old thunder rumbles,
happy, in pulsing brasses. The small
eddies play in the stones sidling close
to islets estranged from the shore. Sirens
call from ominous rocks, flutelike voices
pierce sailors, oboes circle their waists
with longing, gulls laugh, raucous,
swallows loop over the water's edge.
The winds tease and jumble. Aeolus smiles,
taking pleasure in power under wraps.
Tomorrow: tsunami.

War

On Hearing Shostakovich's *Piano Trio #3* (1944)

I never suffered it
but his warped, brooding tunes
make me know it
as surely as Emily knew her moor.
I hear it in the family stories:
the moldy sawdust bread
bought with wheelbarrows of money
that my father, a child in Germany,
balled and threw against a wall
where it stuck, and his mother cried.

My Italian mother-in-law couldn't
throw out the most threadbare
piece of clothing. It's new,
she said, because then
clothes were not allowed a moment's
mourning before being pressed
into service on a new, live body.

In the drumbeat of soldiers
I hear Uncle Friedrich, the goalie
on the hometown team —
he's mourning his fleetest forward
who returned without a leg.
Later, he shot himself.
And before, what must he have whispered,
clinging in the night to his wife,

and what hidden, not to frighten her
or the children—always the children,
Shostakovich tells us, *pizzicato*,
caught in the middle.

The Poet's Improbable Wand

Pick an object, any object.
Examine its soul, its companions.

Try a sack, any sack—
sack of gold, sack of spuds,
wino's sack, Sack of Rome.

Now dig deeper. Find
the birth sac,
bag lady, sackcloth and ashes.

Sacks balloon, collapse
like the belly.
Think of Africa, sacked again and again
where the bellies swell
        with emptiness.

The picture fades.
        I drop my wand.
        Nothing has changed—yet.

        Poor wizard I. Try again.

IV. Inner Darkness, Inner Light

Stillness

When I sit still as dry bones,
I feel the earth tremble
ever so slightly beneath my feet.
Perhaps it is the pushing out
of the gnarled roots of my big maples
or the burrowing of insect armies.
Or perhaps a faraway fault line
slips out to me, so full
myself of fault lines—as old
china displays the thin lines
of its long endurance.
Then I know
everything is in motion.
Everything.

Escape Hatch

for Carlo & Ro

There is no now like the night
for endurance in the mind.
It lies: time will always be like this,
uniform, empty.
The awakened mind is unreined
in its canter across embroidered
fields of perhaps.
Time is finally a rubber band,
and the day's mail slots of hours
with their parceled tasks are banished.
Life's lottery spins on somewhere else
until the scrim of dawn rises
and—Gotcha!—
the stage manager
thrusts us out into the play
with our lines, few or many,
waiting to be said.

Signs

The first signs—simple aberrations, yes?
They come and go, never quite defined.
The light plays like a dirge when you can't guess

the winding truth that seeps, ambiguous,
like chilly winds through cracks you just can't find.
The first signs—simple aberrations, yes?

Once placid faces mirror your distress—
your friends to speculation are inclined.
The light becomes a dirge when you can't guess

the cipher that your body's cells possess.
True and false seem utterly entwined.
The first signs—simple aberrations, yes?

Constant worry makes the self obsess;
days limp or skitter, deadlines left behind.
The light plays like a dirge when you can't guess

what's next in this demonic game of chess,
as poor self falters in the jungle of the mind.
The first signs—simple aberrations, yes?
The light plays like a dirge when you can't guess.

Conjuring

The Ibo tribe in the dead of night
calls a snake a string
so it will not hear its name
and come, slithering.

What shall I call the snakes that stalk
me, beady-eyed, malign?
Could I translate out their power,
mint terror's anodyne?

I fumble in my pouch of words
desperate to find
the coin to charm the evil out
of names that chill my mind.

No luck. Those snakes have come before
and surely will return,
my modern spells and amulets
fool's gold in ancient urns.

Acts

I unsheathe a pen—
nothing more.
And yet behind the mind's curtain
I hear whispers of another
deadly disrobing.

They came to America,
Fukuichi and Kikuko Nakada,
to place food under the tree
where her blood first fell.
They sat at the trial of her killer
to learn how it happened
so they could tell her all,
the all
that blanched into grief,
charred into ash,
all memory's meanings darkened
like photos snatched from flames.

Was it a crookedness
behind his eyes?
When her body was stripped by fire,
his warp was bared—
it glistened like his knife
in ghastly light.

Give me a reason for acts
that change the meaning
of all the others.

Hospital Cruise

My dear, I took a cruise
to the far corners of the world
from my hospital bed.
We stopped for several days in Iran.
I saw no mosques,
no crowds of men
shouting and shaking their fists,
but I tasted the cookies
made with nuts and honey.
I learned of medicinal herbs
from a homesick healer
lying in the bed beside me
and through her longing,
her family as guides,
I toured the countryside,
climbed towering Mount Damavand,
its beeches and oaks
running down the slopes
to the Caspian Sea.

I nodded into naps
my dreams woven
in exotic strands of Farsi.

In that voyage
we made other ports of call —
to Anesthesia, Recovery —

pain sometimes swam alongside,
an octopus with long tentacles.
I remember rescues by strong hands
from Sierra Leone, Liberia, Ivory Coast,
kindness from India,
Ghana's gentle sadness.

So many people, so far from home.

Some days we stopped in the Caribbean
where I dreamed of jerk and ginger.
On Haiti's day I trotted out
my rusty French
and made some headway.

Then Jamaica
brought gusts of laughter on board.

      But always the oceans rose
huge in my mind
bottle green to turquoise,
their waves singing
and slapping
of a sunny morning,
moaning in rain.

A fresh swirl of accents, a new port?
Madagascar? No, Miami!
Soon, Baltimore, and I'll be home.

The Dream Sloop

You sail for us in the wind-loving sloop,
your agile limbs scrambling over the boards
as a spider, its line swinging, ambles its loop
of web. You drink deeply of sun and hoard
it's glory, dive and swim, a true water sprite.
The night sky, its swarm of stars, fills your eyes
with wonder, the whitecaps clap their delight
while in the trailing wake, butterflies
of phosphorescent light will swirl as we glide,
a mirror to stars as we shadow you.
The wind may sing of solitude, but always
others, who cannot make the journey, ride
your decks and pull your ropes, invisible crew
filling the silence with longing—stowaways.

It

She saw her loss, watching from the corner.
She kept it there, half-wild, half tame,
only loosing it at night or it would roam
her dreams, seeking revenge. She knew
deep down she couldn't free it during the day—
it would make her clocks run backward,
her milk turn sour. Plus, it wanted
delicacies: truffles and wild strawberries
while she lived on spinach and cheese.

Sometimes it moaned and scratched
so loud she had to take it out to walk,
no matter where, leashed of course—
the neighbors would nod and smile
that sad smile. Some would turn away.

No sooner they came to a deserted field
or empty lot, she let it loose,
hoping no one would hear its screams
until it returned, docile to the leash.
It never left her. She thought: maybe time
will tame it, if I can't, who knows?
And so the days turned and the seasons.

A Call to the Florist
when X did not succeed in suicide

Had they a cyclamen to send,
I might have written:
"Life is fragile like this bloom."
Had they a Delft vase of bulbs:
"Water these and life will come
as from the womb."
If just geraniums were left:
"Life is sturdy like these petals
barely tousled by the wind's breath."

Had they only roses, I might have said:
"Life is always a romance with death."
But I did not know what flower to seek
any more than I know what life really is.
And so I wrote:
"No words. Just let the flowers speak."

Elegy for a Lost Toe

I paid little mind
to this humble familiar,
one of ten,
now the third to go.

This little piggy brought me
the first pinch of love.
It taught me
the real numbers,
the bottom line of floor,
the mystery of earth,
the pain of thorn and gravel.

Now it teaches me
the numbness of death
and how much
I have yet to lose.

Of Saints and Sinners

It's so much a matter of degree.
Most of us garden variety folk
are made from the if and when
of life's whole cloth,
woven from reverence
to cussing piss and vinegar.
As for walking the walk,
we meander like old rivers
whose paths are looped and leveled.

The *real* sinners turn our marrow to wax,
our feet to jelly—Hitler, Stalin, Pol Pot,
James Jones, Karadic—their siblings
are legion. They bloody our dreams,
blacken our suns. Molochs reborn,
their maws grind children to pulp.

The saints we admire
(from a distance, for they burn)
make good by grasping tight
the upper border of the cloth
where the weave melts into pure light.
They see the whole fabric,
with its rents and tears, its stains
of love and lust, but from afar,
as a bell-ringer sees the countyside

all around the belfry,
the farms and factories,
the necessary bugs pinging
against the beauty, making
sense of the mire
into which the foot
                    so easily slips.

Gathering Together/Holding Firm *

Can it be true? The time of obstruction
is passed, says the Oracle. The obstacles
were so many, an avalanche of stones
each holding its separate peril.
Having survived them,
they become the mountain of my strength.
I will turn each over to learn its secrets
and from the combat
of the devils and angels within it,
I will learn stillness and grace,
the power of a stone at rest.

*A chapter title in the *I Ching*.

Don't

Don't send me flowers
for love or grief—
their slashed green stalks
only tell me how death
came in their cutting,
how the color of each petal
hides its demise, its lost root
gone like the wife of the man
on a roof in New Orleans,
who cries out, over and over,
to the camera and the world
how the storm snatched her
right out of his hands,
how he could not hold her
against that hellish wind.

Give me instead a plant
that still has hope of life—
a cyclamen, an amaryllis,
a cactus that flowers and stabs—
like truth.

Always the Trains

I. They rumble through my mind,
one of them always leaving somewhere.

Once the long whistle
opened for me a space of pure being
between lists and laundry.
My dreams sneaked on board,
checked the compartments for spies
and counterspies, then returned
to my pockets, pondering.

II. The coffee pots in the dining car
gleamed silver sparks of morning.
The biscuits, slathered with butter
and jam, jumped to our mouths.
All night we had rocked in our berths,
the sea calling us in sleep, its waves
rushing to meet us, our bamboo
suitcases, the first we owned, near
bursting, snatches of color peeking
between branches cut to serve the yen
to travel, ready to leap with us
to the platform.

       We would go down
beneath the sea stacks, down where
the frenzy of life swirled in the wet sand

and ebb tide oozed between our toes,
leaving behind clams and crabs.
We would swim and dry and swim
and make love, the cormorants calling,
until, sun and sea bleached, it was time
to return to the train, its whistle
promising, promising.

III. Sometimes the wheels of a train
drone the Unspeakable Loss.
I want to jump the train, roll
down the embankment, escape
as They did not.

Other times the wheels carry the sadness
of those I put outside my field of vision.
The trains cross that field and reveal them all—
with the sedge, the poppies and the old weeds
tangled like the hair of a sick woman.

On good days they haul away worries, free me
to see what is behind my eyes—the lotus
whose petals open and close with my breath.

IV. Always the trains, rattling past grimy windows
and sooty bricks, past antebellum porches,
shuttling past fields where cows sleep on their feet,
sheep bundle to a brook, past places
where people's longing plays out
between stained sheets
and mint tea or shots of whiskey,
framed between the whistle of one 5:19
and the next. The trains shuttle crates
of stories but turn them all
into a twisting tale of staying or leaving.

Now they blurt warnings
and my dreams scurry back in boxcars.

Yet somewhere a train is always arriving,
carrying tinker toys and bridge beams, coffins and wombs.

About the Author

JUDY NERI loves to find hers and others' poems in books, in office buildings, on benches, in music and in the dust on her bureau. She has placed in *The Formalist* and *Passager* (2002 and 2006) contests, and had poems in *The Lyric*, *Poet Lore*, *Potomac Review*, *Innisfree* and many other reviews. One of her poems was read by Garrison Keillor on NPR's The Writer's Almanac. She has poems in three anthologies and one on a bench in Bethesda. Many of her poems have been displayed in the Montgomery County Poets' Gallery at the Executive Office Building in Rockville, Maryland. She has a Ph.D. in Comparative Literature from the University of Maryland. She writes essays as well, most recently on the arts, and has worked as a college teacher and labor editor.

Printed in the United States
203931BV00005B/7-9/A

9 780980 081411